How do I use this scheme?

Key Words with Peter and Jane has three parallel series, each containing twelve books. All three series are written using the same carefully controlled vocabulary. Readers will get the most out of **Key Words** with Peter and Jane when they follow the books in the pattern 1a, 1b, 1c; 2a, 2b, 2c and so on.

• Series a
gradually introduces and repeats new words.

• Series b
provides further practice of these same words, but in a different context and with different illustrations.

• Series c
uses familiar words to teach **phonics** in a methodical way, enabling children to read increasingly difficult words. It also provides a link to writing.

LADYBIRD BOOKS

UK | USA | Canada | Ireland | Australia
India | New Zealand | South Africa

Ladybird Books is part of the Penguin Random House group of companies
whose addresses can be found at global.penguinrandomhouse.com.

www.penguin.co.uk   www.puffin.co.uk   www.ladybird.co.uk

First published 1964
This edition 2009, 2014, 2016
Copyright © Ladybird Books Ltd, 1964
001

A CIP catalogue record for this book is
available from the British Library

ISBN: 978-1-409-30113-4

Printed in China

Key Words

with Peter and Jane

3a   Things we like

written by W. Murray
illustrated by M. Aitchison

Here are Peter and Jane.

They like to play.

Up they go.

Up, up, up, they go.

I like this, says Peter.
It is fun.

Pat the dog wants to play.

---

new words

play   up

Jane and Peter like
to play.

Here they are at play.

I go up, up, up, says Jane.

I go down, down, down,
says Peter.

Up and down, up and down,
up and down we go.

---

new words

at   down

Jane and Peter play
in the water.

They like to play
on the boat.

Come on, says Peter.

Come on the boat.

Come and play on the boat.

Jump up.   Jump up here.

---

new words

on   boat

Jane is in the water and
Peter is in the boat.

They want to fish.

Peter can see a fish
in the water.

Get in the boat, says Peter.

The fish can see you
in the water.

Get in the boat, Jane.

---

new words

see   Get   get

Look at me, says Peter.

Look at me, Jane.

Look at me in the boat.

Come on, he says.

Come and play in the boat,
Jane.

Come on, Pat.

---

new word

me

I want a cake, please,
says Peter.

A cake for me, please,
he says.

Here you are, says Jane.

Here are some cakes.

A cake for you and
a cake for me.

I like cakes and you like
cakes.

---

new words

cake   please

Here is the station.

Peter and Jane are at
the station.

They like the station.

The train comes in.

Look at the train,
says Peter.

See the train, Jane.

I like trains, he says.

new words

station   train

Peter likes to play
with toys.

He plays with a toy station
and a toy train.

Jane says, Please can I play?

Please can I play with you?

Yes, says Peter. I have
the train.

You play with the station.

---

new word

with

Here is the shop.

Peter and Jane look at
the dogs.

They look at the rabbits.

Look at this one,
says Peter.

This is the one we want.

Yes, this is the one.

We want this rabbit.

---

new words

rabbits   one

Peter and Jane go into
the shop.

We want that rabbit,
says Peter to the man.

Yes, that one, please.

Here you are, says the man.

Here it is, he says.

new words

that   man

Jane and Peter like to help Mummy.

They go to the shops for Mummy.

I like to shop, says Jane. It is fun.

Come on, Peter says. We have to go to the fish shop.

Yes, says Jane. It helps Mummy.

new words

help   Mummy

Peter and Jane like to help Daddy.

They help Daddy with the car.

Jane is in the car.

Daddy and Peter have some water.

Peter likes to play with water.

I like it, he says. It is fun.

---

new words

Daddy   car

Here they go, in the car.

Daddy is in the car with Peter and Jane.

We like it in the car, they say.

Go on, Daddy, go on.

We want to go on and on.

This is good fun, they say.

---

new word

good

Look, Jane, that is a
Police car.

It says POLICE on it.

That is the Police Station.

I like the Police, says Peter.
They help you.

Yes, says Jane. The Police
help you.

---

new words

Police   POLICE

Here is an apple tree.

Apples are good for you,
says Peter.

Have an apple, Jane.

An apple for you and
an apple for me.

Mummy wants some and
we want some.

No, Pat, no apples for you.

---

new words

an   apple

Peter and Jane are
at home.

They play with the rabbit.

They like to see the rabbit
jump.

Give it an apple, says Peter.

No, says Jane. Give it
some water.

The man in the shop says
it wants water.

---

new words

Give   give

Here are some trees and flowers.

Jane and Peter want some flowers.

Some flowers for you and some for me, says Jane.

Get some flowers, Peter.

Get some for Mummy and get some for Daddy.

---

new word

flowers

The man in the shop likes Jane and Peter, and they like the man.

He has the apples they like.

We want the red ones, please, they say.

Get the red ones, please.

---

new word

red

Peter has the red ball.

He plays with the boys with the red ball.

Jane looks on.

That was good, Peter, says Jane. That was good.

The boys say, Yes, Peter, that was good.

Good for you.

---

new words

boys   was

See the bus, Peter.

See the red bus.

The boys and the girls are in the bus.

Come on, Peter, says Jane.

We have to get in.

The boys and the girls like the bus.

It is fun in the bus.

---

new words

bus   girls

The boys and girls
go to school.

They go to school
in the bus.

The boys and girls like to
go to school in the bus.

They have fun in the bus.

They like the bus and
they like school.

---

new word

school

Some boys and girls come to tea.

They come to tea with Jane and Peter.

Jane helps Mummy with the tea.

Jane gives the girls tea, and Peter gives the boys cakes.

They like to have boys and girls to tea.

new word

tea

Up to bed, Jane,
says Mummy.

Up to bed, Peter,
says Daddy.

Up to bed you go.

Yes, say Peter and Jane.
We want to go to bed.

It was fun in the water,
says Peter.

Yes, says Jane, and it
was fun at tea.

---

new word

bed

a rabbit

a boat

an apple

a cake

a car

the red bus

a man

the school

some boys

some girls

the train

a bed

some flowers

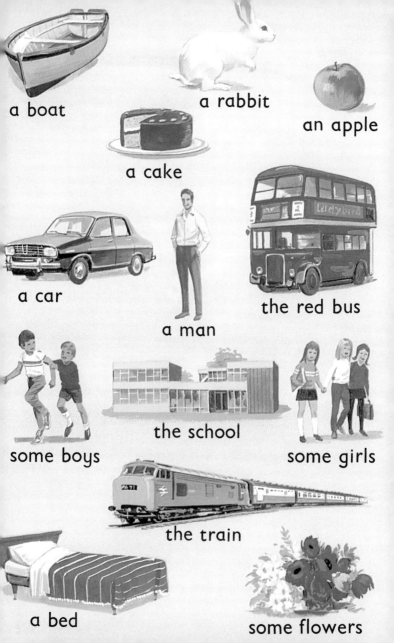

a boat

a rabbit

an apple

a cake

a car

a man

the red bus

some boys

the school

some girls

the train

a bed

some flowers

New words used in this book

Total number of new words: 36
Average repetition per word: 11